PASSING THE BATON
PLANNING FOR PASTORAL TRANSITION

"Leadership change can be one of the most painful or fulfilling experiences a leader can encounter. In *Passing the Baton*, Dr. Terry Roberts helps us through this process. It is by far the best document I have read on this subject. A must read."
Pastor Tommy Barnett, Founder of Los Angeles and Phoenix Dream Centers

"The book *Passing the Baton* by Dr. Terry Roberts is long overdue. This concise, user friendly manual will provide a pastor or church board a strategy to give guidance in one of the major changes that every church will face in its lifetime, a pastoral transition."
Rev. Victor Smith, Superintendent, South Carolina District Assemblies of God

"In *Passing the Baton*, Dr. Terry Roberts provides an invaluable and practical guide for pastors and congregations as they face the inevitable need to plan for transition in their pastoral leadership. I strongly and highly recommend it as a resource."
Alonzo Johnson, Ph.D., Superintendent, Church of God in Christ, South Carolina Jurisdiction

"This book is a must-read for all ministry leaders who wish to steward their calling, ministry and organization with excellence. Terry Roberts tackles the tough issues of pastoral transition and offers a clear guide to navigating this—potentially turbulent—season of leadership with a high degree of excellence and confidence. *Passing the Baton* of leadership to the emerging generation of ministry leaders can be navigated with assurance and conviction when we apply the wisdom of this book to a season of transition. I know this book will have a great impact among ministry leaders."
Dr. Kent Ingle, President, Southeastern University, Lakeland, Florida

"*Passing the Baton: Planning for Pastoral Transition* is such a fine work for local church boards, pulpit committees, and congregational insights. It represents a perfect resource for churches whose methods for seeking spiritual leadership for their pulpits, as well as top tier posts, need clarifying and finding a wise focus for searching out these often times elusive leaders. I appreciate the words: "A true church is more than an organization; it is a living organism pulsating with the life of God!" Any congregation and its internal leadership who embrace that essential idea will have, at its root, the makings of a Holy Spirit led direction. Terry Roberts has brought that message into sharp focus in this book. He has thought it through, and for those who read it and take it to heart, their lives will be forever changed as a result."
Rev. T. Ray Rachels, Executive Presbyter, General Council of the Assemblies of God

"Pastors planning to retire or transition are wise to put Terry Roberts' concise book on pastoral transition into every leader's hand. Pastoral succession shouldn't be disruptive to the congregation. Here's how to avoid a heart-wrenching crisis."
Rev. Ed Nelson, Executive Secretary-Treasurer, South Carolina District Assemblies of God

"Upon receiving Dr. Terry Roberts' book, *Passing the Baton*, I recommended it to the president and four other regional directors of Open Bible Churches. Its concise and relevant writing makes it a 'must read' for every leader interested in finding the right successor in leadership transition."
Dr. Jim Beaird, Executive Director, Southeast Region, Open Bible Churches

"In *Passing the Baton,* Terry Roberts has addressed an area that is critical to finishing well. This is a great resource for any pastor or leader. It presents a compelling case for planning for leadership transition, and it includes practical ideas for making it work."
Pastor Ken Owen, First Assembly of God, Greenville, SC and Assistant Superintendent, South Carolina District of the Assemblies of God

"*Passing the Baton* is probably the most practical and helpful book I've read in quite some time. Your work is excellent and is very helpful to me as I work through plans at Christian Life."
Dr. Stephen Chitty, Lead Pastor, Christian Life Church, Columbia, South Carolina

"*Passing the Baton: Planning for Pastoral Transition* brings focus to an often neglected area of pastoral ministry that is important for the long-term success of a church and to help the fruit of a Pastor remain."
Rev. Phil Simun, Presbyter, South Carolina District Assemblies of God

"Thousands of churches have suffered greatly from well-meaning, but mismanaged, pastoral transition. What often seems the best way to select a new pastor can lead to deep conflict, resentment, and a loss of effective ministry. Dr. Terry Roberts has used extensive research in conjunction with a lifetime of ministry leadership experience to lay out a clear and healthy model for church transition that is an essential tool for those on both sides of the interview table. I highly encourage church boards, denominational leaders, and pastors to carefully read and follow Roberts' approach detailed in this excellent book."
Dr. Alan Ehler, Dean, College of Christian Ministries and Religion, Southeastern University, Lakeland, Florida

PASSING THE BATON
PLANNING FOR PASTORAL TRANSITION

Terry Roberts, D.Min.

Published by Terrell G. Roberts
Please direct inquiries to TGRoberts@sc.rr.com

Passing the Baton: Planning for Pastoral Transition
Copyright © 2015 by Terry Roberts

Requests for information about this book should be addressed to TGRoberts@sc.rr.com

ISBN 13: 978-1515309918

This book is intended as a source of general information on pastoral transition, particularly in autonomous churches with pastor-led or congregational forms of governance. The information contained herein is based on material from other published works, interviews with pastors, and the author's personal experiences in ministry. In no way does the author purport to provide legal or financial advice. Nor does he imply that these concepts will apply to every situation. Readers are encouraged to seek the counsel of their church and/or denominational leaders, as well as professional legal opinions regarding the specifics of their situation.

Cover design by Chris Wallace. Contact: cwallace7@sc.rr.com

Contents

Introduction

"The current model of pastoral transition …
is the organizational equivalent of burning down
the community library every time
a new mayor is elected."
Carolyn Weese and J. Russell Crabtree

"What would you do if I died today?" When Pastor J. Don George posed that question to his younger associate, Ben Dailey, he noted the stunned look in Dailey's eyes. Quickly, George clarified the question: "If I left the scene and you felt completely free to dream and plan with no reservations, what do you think God might lead you to do? How would you change the way ministry is done here at Calvary?" Then George challenged him with these words: "Whatever that vision may be, that's what I want you to do. But don't wait until I'm gone. Let's do it now, and let's do it together."[1] With those words, Don George initiated the pastoral transition at Calvary Church in Irving, Texas. He tells the complete story in his book, *Against the Wind: Creating a Church of Diversity through Authentic Love.*

As founding pastor of Calvary Church, George was a seasoned veteran known for decades of successful leadership at this mega church. More recently, he had helped the church transition from a smug, middle-class congregation to a vibrant, multi-ethnic church reaching their very diverse city. Now, George had come to the realization that his church needed the passion and cultural relevance of a younger leader. He also saw the wisdom of a planned leadership transition. George says, "God's message to me was that I should make room for the ministry of Ben Dailey. God did not tell me to step out or step back. He simply told me to step over and make room. ... I received God's instruction with excitement and enthusiasm."[2]

---

[1] J. Don George, *Against the Wind: Creating a Church of Diversity through Authentic Love* (Springfield, Missouri: My Healthy Church, 2012), Kindle e–book, Location 1791.

[2] Ibid., Kindle e–book, Location 1626.

Dailey had previously been on staff at Calvary Church for seven years, during which time George had mentored him in ministry. Now, George began preparing Dailey to step into the role of Lead Pastor. Today, the two continue serving Calvary Church together. As Lead Pastor, Dailey has the hands-on responsibility of pastoral oversight and leadership. As "Founding Pastor," George remains involved in the life of the church, while enjoying the freedom to minister beyond Calvary.

This successful pastoral transition at Calvary Church, initiated by the veteran pastor, spared the congregation the upheaval that many churches experience when a tenured leader leaves the pulpit. The plan engaged the vision and energy of a younger leader while retaining the wisdom and perspective of the veteran. It injected new life into the church without destroying the existing DNA. As such, it serves as a worthy model for other churches to consider. Unfortunately, it remains a rare exception to the rule.

The Cost of Not Having a Plan

Pastoral changes in many American churches result in confusion and dysfunction. When Pastors move, retire, or die without a successor, congregations flounder. Often the church calls a new pastor, unknown to the congregation, and with little to recommend him beyond his own résumé and a sermon or two. Because the new pastor has no prior experience in the life of the church, the previous vision dies, or it changes so radically that people can't make the shift.

Even if a church manages to get a good replacement pastor, things can happen during the interim that end up tying his hands. For example, lay leaders with ulterior motives can step into the leadership vacuum and implement unhealthy changes in policy or bylaws, or they can become a control clique. Furthermore, the new pastor often must deal with "loyalty conflict" in the congregation, especially when the previous pastor was highly regarded. "Members feel conflicted if [the new pastor] heads in a direction ... the predecessor would not have gone.

The [new pastor] is in competition with a person who is present only in the minds of the people."[3]

Add to this the financial cost to replace a pastor if members leave the church or withhold their contributions. Other costs include honoraria for interim leadership and the expenses of recruiting a new pastor. In their book *Elephant in the Boardroom,* Carolyn Weese and Russell Crabtree observe, "It is accepted as an industry standard that the cost of replacing a professional is roughly equivalent to the annual salary of the position. The cost of replacing a pastor is even higher."[4]

Weese and Crabtree suggest that "every organization has dysfunctional elements; they tend to emerge as a strong leader begins to recede."[5] As a case in point, they cite Jesus' departure from his disciples and the twin crises involving Judas' betrayal and Simon

---

[3] Carolyn Weese and J. Russell Crabtree, *The Elephant in the Boardroom: Speaking the Unspoken about Pastoral Transitions* (San Francisco, CA: Jossey-Bass, 2004), Kindle e–book, Location 805.

[4] Ibid., Kindle e–book, Location 352.

[5] Ibid., Kindle e–book, Location 320.

Peter's denial. "Rather than seeing this as an odd set of events unique to the Son of God, we should see this as the expected emergence of the dysfunctional side of an organization at a time of leadership transition."[6] In their book, they lament the disruption that afflicts most churches when a pastor leaves:

> The current model of pastoral transition, left over from a time when organizational learning was not as important, does not help congregations protect what is healthy and retain what they have learned. It is the organizational equivalent of burning down the community library every time a new mayor is elected, as if the only information we now need is what the latest mayor brings.[7]

Surely the church can do better than that. There must be a healthier way for churches to handle the challenges of pastoral change. Well, there is indeed, and that is the subject of this little book.

In the pages that follow I will look at various transition models and examine their vital components.

---

[6] Ibid.

[7] Ibid., Kindle e-book, Location 1756.

I will talk about several churches that have navigated transition successfully, and I will tell the story of one notable transition failure. Some of those churches are large, others not so large. Some have a form of governance that allows the lead pastor to appoint his successor. Others follow congregational governance requiring the vote of the membership.

As I will point out, there is no "one-size-fits-all" model. Plans differ, just as the churches they serve differ. However, the best plans have one thing in common: They combine the wisdom and stability of a seasoned leader with the vision and energy of a younger leader. As such, they help the church not only *go* through the challenge of change, but also *grow* through it.

A "Readable" Resource for Churches

The brevity of this book is one of its benefits. A little book better serves as the kind of resource a pastor can put into the hands of his key leaders to begin the process of transition planning. Given the plethora of media options today, getting people to actually read a book can be a daunting challenge. However, a book with 100 pages that can be read in about an hour means people are more apt to read it, and therefore they can approach the process better informed.

Despite its small package, however, this book contains a wealth of information. I have reviewed a considerable amount of contemporary literature on the subject and distilled much of that wisdom here. In citing those works, I have chosen to use footnotes, rather than endnotes, to encourage the reader to identify the sources. I recommend that pastors invest the time reading these lengthier works and, to that end, I provide full publication information in the bibliography.

Beyond studying published works, I have also personally interviewed pastors who have led successful transitions, including Tommy Barnett (see chapter four). Additionally, I have had the privilege of sitting at the feet of leaders in the Asian Church where pastoral transition seems to be more the norm than in America. To the extent that such is possible, the Asian Church has perfected the art of pastoral transition. Their wisdom and experience inform an entire chapter of this book.

Content Overview

In chapter one I discuss the benefits of a transition plan. I will show that having a plan not only makes sense, it is thoroughly biblical. Chapter two takes a look at what the Asian Church has learned about pastoral transition and how their experience could benefit the American Church. In chapter three I tell the story of a successful pastoral transition in a church with congregational governance—the situation in many American churches. Chapter four recounts successful transitions in some larger churches with pastor-led governance. It also contemplates the wisdom of a continuing role for the veteran pastor after the transition. In chapter five, I discuss the essential components of a successful transition, and as a reference point, I tell the painful story of one very visible transition failure. I also discuss some of the financial implications of transition, such as monetary consideration for the retiring veteran. Chapter six addresses the unavoidable turbulence that comes with any major change, especially leadership change. It also shares keys for managing that turbulence along with a few paradoxes about change that seem to defy logic. Chapter seven honestly faces the difficulty of transition planning and suggests a great "first step" to get the ball rolling.

In its current form, this book applies primarily to autonomous churches with pastor-led or congregational forms of governance. For churches belonging to denominations with centralized or hierarchical governance, these principles will need to be adapted and used under the guidance of the bishop or denominational executive. I am indebted to my colleague and friend, Dr. Alonzo Johnson of the Church of God in Christ, for his kind review of this material and his insightful recommendation that a future edition include a chapter addressing the role of denominational hierarchy in the transition process.

Let me also acknowledge those who granted interviews or furnished information about their transitions: Tommy Barnett, David Lim, Ron McGee, and Phil Simun.

I am indebted to Drs. Wayne and Sherry Lee, founders of Church Life Resources, L.L.C. Their keen insights about the Church have seeded my thinking.

The congregation and staff of Trinity Church have loved me and allowed me to serve them for over a quarter of a century. They have taught me much.

Finally, to Sandra, my precious wife of 47 years and my most ardent encourager, thank you!

Terry Roberts
Columbia, South Carolina
October 2015

1

The Wisdom of a Plan

"Wisdom is the principal thing; therefore get wisdom:
and with all thy getting get understanding."
Proverbs 4:7

I first heard the saying from my father-in-law, a successful businessman: "Plan your work, then work your plan." I was a brand-new pastor, and even though I had just spent four years learning about pastoral ministry at Bible College, I was in over my head. That's when my father-in-law offered his well-intended advice. Looking back, if I even comprehended his words, I didn't have a clue about how to apply them to pastoring. I didn't grow up in a pastor's home, so I had little idea of how a pastor spent his time beyond his Sunday duties. Courses on pastoral theology and pastoral counseling led me to believe the needs of the congregation would keep me plenty busy. But, the tiny congregation I led required little of me, and I found myself with loads of time on my hands wondering why the phone didn't ring.

I continued to flounder for my first year of ministry. But, as the Apostle so aptly put it, "The One who calls you is faithful, and He will do it."[8] When I finally cried out to the Lord in desperation, He came to my rescue through an early morning encounter with Him in His Word. From then on, daily meditations in the Bible became my source of joy and fuel for ministry. I had discovered the exquisite beauty of the rose when crowned with the dew of the morning.[9] Following that encounter, I began to function with a measure of confidence and even enjoyment of pastoral ministry, and I experienced fruitfulness. The phone began to ring. And ring.

Nevertheless, in practice my ministry remained more reactive than proactive. I was good at responding to

---

[8] 1 Thessalonians 5:24

[9] See Psalm 110:3. Recall also the words in the first verse of the hymn "In the Garden."

people's needs—at *doing* the work of the ministry—but not so good at equipping them for ministry. I still lacked a plan.

Years later, I ran across this adage: "If you fail to plan, you plan to fail." I began to see that effective pastoral ministry involves more than putting out fires and officiating at rites of passage. It involves more than responding to the needs of parishioners—important as that is. Effective pastors don't sit around waiting for the phone to ring. They help initiate ministry and outreach and structures that not only address the needs of their people but also involve their people in ministry to others. Under God, they move the church forward in strategic ways to new levels of growth and fruitfulness. Effective pastors do indeed plan their work and work their plan.

Jesus counseled his followers to plan. His parables about the man proposing to build a tower and the king expecting to engage an enemy focus on the need to count the cost.[10] Somewhere in that process of

---

[10] Luke 14:28

counting the cost is the need for planning. One cannot imagine a builder undertaking a project of any magnitude without a carefully laid plan including detailed blueprints. Obviously, the more important the project, the more important the plan.

Today, many pastors realize the value of strategic planning for their churches. They guide their staff and key leaders through annual calendar planning exercises and long-range planning that establishes mission, casts vision, sets goals, and determines methodologies for reaching them. In so doing, they demonstrate proactive, strategic leadership.

Yet, when it comes to leadership transition, pastors often fail to plan. For example, how many pastors who leave one church for another first set in place a plan of action for those they leave behind? How many pastors approaching retirement age have initiated a dialogue with their lay leaders about a successor? How many churches have a crisis transition plan to guide them if the unexpected happens, like the untimely death or disability of their pastor? (None of us like to think of such things, yet in our more rational moments we know they can happen. That's why we carry life insurance.) Peter Drucker, the famous management guru revered in the world of corporate business, laments that "the ingredient most missing in churches today is a plan of succession."[11]

The Only Thing Constant...

Pastors and churches demonstrate great wisdom when they work together to develop a plan for leadership transition. For one thing, leadership change is inevitable. No one lives forever. No one is viable forever. And, beyond health concerns, older pastors face other challenges. The culture around the church undergoes perpetual change. Younger generations are continually rising, looking for younger leaders who know their culture, speak their language, and understand their perspective on life. The church needs the forward-leaning vision of younger pastors.

On the other hand, the church also needs the wisdom and stability that seasoned pastors offer. When older

---

[11] Bob Russell and Bryan Bucher, *Transition Plan* (Louisville, KY: Ministers Label Publishing, 2010), 18.

members of the congregation feel unsettled by the creativity and cultural relevance of a younger pastor, the presence of the veteran pastor can buffer the turmoil. Furthermore, the veteran's wealth of pastoral experience can position him or her to serve as a mentor to the successor.

Regarding the role of mentor, Wayne and Sherry Lee, founders of Church Life Resources, L.L.C., underscore the importance of a mentor or coach for every pastor. In their book, *The Church Life Model: A Biblical Pattern for the Spirit-filled Church,* the Lees state: "The genius and skill of leading a congregation to grow requires a strong relationship with Christ, knowledge, experience, and *dynamic reflection with a coach or mentor* (emphasis added)."[12] The Lees mention the payback pastors receive when they demonstrate the courage and humility to reflect on their leadership practices with a mentor. This is a benefit that comes as "standard equipment" with a good pastoral transition plan. There are also other

---

[12] Wayne Lee and Sherry Lee, *The Church Life Model: A Biblical Pattern for the Spirit-filled Church* (Lake Mary, FL: Creation House, 2011), 42.

benefits to consider.

Benefits of a Transition Plan

When pastors and churches intentionally confront the "elephant" of pastoral transition, not only do they avoid some of the pitfalls cited earlier, they also reap a number of benefits:

1) They ensure continuity of vision from one administration to another. This is especially true when the successor has been a part of the church for several years.

2) They uncork the creative potential of younger leaders and inject youthful vision and energy into the life of the church.

3) They stabilize the congregation, lessening the upheaval of major change.

4) They help bridge the "generation gap." Some young people regard an older leader as "out of touch" because of his age. However, by elevating a younger leader to a higher role, the church continues to engage and inspire young people. On the other hand, when older members of the congregation feel alienated by the change of leadership, the veteran can

encourage their patience and continued support. Considering that much of the revenue comes from older members, this can involve significant financial benefit to the church.

5) Succession opens another chapter of meaningful ministry to the veteran leader. Having handed off the burden of church management, he can establish a greater legacy as a fathering mentor to younger leaders or as a consultant to other pastors and churches.

A Matter of Common Sense

The business world has long understood the need to plan for leadership succession. In their book, *Transition Plan*, Bob Russell and Bryan Bucher point out that Jack Welch, the famed CEO of General Electric, once commented, "From now on, [choosing my successor] is the most important decision I'll make. It occupies a considerable amount of time every day."[13] Russell and Bucher note that Welch made that statement in 1991, nine years before his retirement. While such planning is no guarantee of a

---

[13] Russell and Bucher, *Transition Plan*, 112.

failure-proof transition, it goes a long way toward easing the stress of such a major change.

In the Church, however, a pastor is sometimes criticized if he attempts to "anoint his own successor." In churches with a congregational polity, the members are accustomed to choosing the new leader, and the outgoing pastor may risk their ire if he even recommends a candidate. Perhaps for this reason, "when it comes to dealing with pastoral transition, many strong leaders stop leading."[14]

This need not be. A good transition plan can unite pastor and people. The pastor can select and mentor a qualified candidate, bringing the congregation into the process through teaching, communication, and ultimately, by their vote of approval. In chapter three, I will tell the story of a pastor and church that did exactly that.

---

[14] Weese and Crabtree, *The Elephant in the Boardroom*, Kindle e–book, Location 75.

A Biblical Approach

The concept of a pastor mentoring and grooming a younger apprentice for his job is not only a matter of common sense, it is biblical.

When Moses learned that he would not lead Israel into Canaan, he immediately prayed for a successor: "O Lord, please appoint a new man as leader ... so the community of the Lord will not be like sheep without a shepherd" (Num. 27:15-17 NLT). The Lord instructed Moses to appoint his assistant Joshua, the man he had mentored for nearly forty years (Ex. 34:9). David named Solomon as his successor (1 Chron. 28:5,6), cast vision for him (1 Chron. 28:9,10), and laid the groundwork for his future success (1 Chron. 28:11-12).[15] Elijah anointed Elisha to assume his prophetic office (I Kings 19:19-21). Paul fathered his son in the faith, so Timothy would be prepared to succeed him (2 Tim. 2:2). In fact, Paul bequeathed his apostolic leadership to Timothy in no uncertain terms:

---

[15] Russell and Bucher, *Transition Plan*, 112.

> I'm passing this work on to you, my son
> Timothy. The prophetic word that was
> directed to you prepared us for this. All those
> prayers are coming together now so you will
> do this well, fearless in your struggle, keeping
> a firm grip on your faith and on yourself
> (1 Tim. 1:18-19 MSG).

On the other hand, the consequences of failing to provide a successor are also apparent in Scripture. Take for example, the case of Joshua and the generation that followed him. How ironic that after serving as Moses' assistant and successor, Joshua died without a successor. Was this a factor in the spiritual failure of the next generation? The book of Judges sadly reports that

> "the people served the Lord all the days of
> Joshua and all the days of the elders who
> outlived Joshua who had seen all the great
> works of the Lord. ... After that generation
> died, another generation grew up who did not
> acknowledge the Lord. ... They abandoned
> the Lord, the God of their ancestors" (Judges
> 2:7-12 NKJV and NLT).

To be sure, Joshua served his generation well. But is it possible that the next generation "abandoned the Lord" because Joshua did not prepare a "next generation leader" to step into his shoes? According to the book of Judges, after Joshua's death, there was no central leader and no cohesive, guiding vision to unite the people. They were "sheep without a shepherd," and consequently, "all the people did what seemed right in their own eyes" (Judges 17:6 NLT). The results were repeated cycles of idolatry, oppression, and defeat. Mercifully, God raised up local leaders from time to time, but the overall picture in Judges is one of spiritual dysfunction.

These biblical examples confirm John Maxwell's famous statement, "There is no success without a successor."[16]

Speaking of John Maxwell, I remember hearing him speak at a church growth conference years ago where he put forth the idea of "working yourself out of a job." He based the concept on the biblical principle in Ephesians 4:11,12:

> It was he who gave some to be apostles, some to be prophets, some to be evangelists, and some to be pastors and teachers, *to prepare God's people for works of service*, so that the

---

[16] Gene Wilkes, *Jesus on Leadership* (Wheaton, IL: Tyndale House, 1998), 208.

body of Christ may be built up (emphasis mine.)

Maxwell explained that a pastor's job is not only to *do* ministry, but to equip others to do ministry— effectively working oneself out of a job.

When Maxwell would hire a new staff pastor, he would tell him at the outset that his main job was to equip the people of the church to do his ministry. Maxwell would say to the new pastor, "I'll give you one year to work yourself out of a job. If you do that, I'll give you another job. If you don't, you may not have a job."[17] Of course, Maxwell applied this biblical principle to pastors equipping the laity, but shouldn't it also apply to the senior pastor equipping a successor?

Pastors do their churches an immense favor when they proactively plan for pastoral change. They also pay themselves a huge compliment by demonstrating effective leadership through one of the most difficult phases of a church's life.

---

[17] My paraphrase based on my memory of Maxwell's comment.

Transition planning is beneficial because it is biblical and because it is a common-sense approach to the inevitable. With that in mind, every lead pastor should pray the prayer Moses prayed: "O Lord, please appoint a new man as leader for the community ... so the community of the Lord will not be like sheep without a shepherd" (Num. 27:15-17 NLT).

If we're open to learning from Christians of a slightly different culture, the Asian Church has much to say to us on this subject, as we shall see in the next chapter.

2

The Asian Model

"The veteran leader positions the younger one, by way of association and affirmation. This association of an older minister standing with the younger one will drastically shorten the time needed for the younger one to build a reputation of his/her own."
Naomi Dowdy

Churches in some parts of the world appear to be ahead of the American Church when it comes to pastoral succession. During my doctoral studies, a course on apostolic leadership involved a trip to Singapore, where our cohort studied characteristics of the Asian Church. Singapore is a modern city-state occupying an island at the southern tip of the Malay Peninsula. It boasts a robust economy, modern amenities, and a culture similar in many ways to Western culture.

Our host and professor was Dr. David Lim, pastor of Singapore's 4,000-member Grace Assembly of God. Lim identified eight major traits of the Singaporean Church: 1) emphasis on spiritual warfare, 2) charismatic leadership, 3) spiritual and structural authority of the apostolic leader, 4) apostolic congregations who influence positive transformation of their culture, 5) missional thrust, 6) proactive exercise of spiritual gifts, 7) the fathering, mentoring role of the apostle, and 8) a model for pastoral succession.[18]

Lim says that true, apostolic leaders carry a trans-generational burden for the ministries they oversee. Realizing they will not always be the senior leader, they seek to develop successors to whom they can pass the baton of leadership. Fathering involves more than merely grooming a younger man for a job. The goal of the veteran leader is to reproduce himself in other leaders (2 Tim. 2:2). That process is highly

---

[18] David Lim, Syllabus and Class notes, PTH L 967 Apostolic Leadership in Asian Churches, Assemblies of God Theological Seminary extension, Singapore, October, 2011, 1.

relational, hence the term "fathering." Paul the Apostle spoke of this when he wrote to the Corinthian church: "Even though you have ten thousand guardians in Christ, you do not have many fathers, for in Christ Jesus I became your father through the gospel" (1 Cor. 4:15-16).

In order for pastoral succession to work effectively, certain steps must be taken to safeguard the process and prepare the congregation for the transition. The Singaporean church provides excellent examples of this process. Trinity Christian Centre is a case in point.

Trinity Christian Centre

For decades, Assemblies of God missionary Naomi Dowdy pastored this church. Under her dynamic leadership, it grew from 42 to 4,600 members.[19] In 1980 a nineteen-year-old man, recently saved from his prodigal lifestyle, began attending the church.

---

[19] Naomi Dowdy, *Moving On and Moving Up from Success to Significance: Practical Principles for Legacy Management and Leadership* (Lake Mary, FL: Creation House, 2010), 7.

Dominic Yeo's passion over his new-found love for Christ caught Dowdy's attention, and she directed him into a cell group, where he was discipled. In time his devotion and diligence were rewarded with the opportunity to lead his own cell group. Yeo joined the church staff as a youth pastor in 1985 and has served in various roles since then, including directing some of the church's major outreach events. In 2005 Dowdy installed Yeo as "Senior Pastor and Apostle" of Trinity Christian Centre. She remains available to Yeo and the church as a mentor/advisor, but now moves in an apostolic anointing, circulating among other churches that look to her for oversight.

The transition from Dowdy to Yeo involved a long process that began even before Yeo came to Trinity. In the early days of Trinity's history, God began prompting Dowdy to involve other preachers in the pulpit ministry. She recalls Him saying to her, "It is not good that the church is growing on your pulpit ministry. It is time to change."[20] Dowdy trained and developed a preaching team which "launched [them]

---

[20] Ibid.

into a whole new phase of development within the church."[21] It also helped prepare her and the church for the ultimate transition from her pastoral leadership.

By the time she was ready to consider pastoral succession, a number of capable leaders in the church were on her short list, Yeo among them. But the decision did not come quickly or easily. It involved years of prayer and soul-searching. "I cannot overstate the need and importance of prayer in this process. You must pray and hear what the Holy Spirit is saying until you can confidently declare: 'We prayed—and it seemed good to the Holy Spirit to set aside [Yeo] for the work to which God has called him.'"[22] Dowdy also encourages that ample time be given to the process. She recommends five to eight years from initial prayer and selection of a successor to completion of the transition.[23]

---

[21] Ibid.

[22] Ibid., 83.

[23] Ibid., 10.

Dowdy tells the complete story of their transition in her book, *Moving On and Moving Up from Succession to Significance*, a valuable resource for those considering pastoral succession. She cautions senior leaders that failure to implement pastoral transition can stifle the leadership growth of subordinates and become a bottleneck to the progress of the church. On the other hand, a well-executed transition can ignite the growth potential of the new leader and the church. Their transition demonstrates this truth. Under Yeo's leadership, Trinity Christian Centre has grown to more than 8,000 members.

A Broader Ministry for the Veteran

Dowdy also believes God has a higher calling for veteran leaders—perhaps broader, apostolic purposes—that can only be realized as the veteran leader transitions out of day-to-day, hands-on leadership and allows the apprentice to assume those roles. Seasoned leaders should consider the possibility that their wisdom could be invested in places beyond their own church. They are a gold mine of information, experience, and encouragement that young pastors fresh from seminary are craving. They can serve as mentors to these young pastors and as consultants to their churches. They can invest relationally and benefit the Kingdom enormously. Simply put, veteran leaders are too valuable an asset to confine to one congregation. Yet, when they continue to carry the daily burden of local church leadership and administration, the constraints of time and waning energy leave little to invest elsewhere. Set free from that daily burden, they can ascend to greater levels of influence for the sake of the Kingdom.

By "moving on and moving up" veteran pastors also enable the growth and development of their own subordinates in ministry. On this matter, Dowdy gets right to the point: "Those serving under you cannot rise to a higher level until you get out of the way."[24] She recommends "a transfer of trust, respect, and confidence—relational capital, if you like—that is passed on to, and inherited by, the new and younger

---

[24] Ibid., 17.

leader. The veteran leader positions the younger one, by way of association and affirmation. This association of an older minister standing with the younger one will drastically shorten the time needed for the younger one to build a reputation of his/her own."[25]

Pastoral succession does far more than stabilize a congregation during a change of leadership. It offers immediate benefit to the veteran and successor and potentially, to many others beyond their local church. More importantly, it establishes a Kingdom-oriented legacy of pastoral ministry.

Grace Assembly of God

This transfer of "relational capital" is precisely what occurred at Singapore's Grace Assembly in 2012. Pastor David Lim realized years before that Calvin Lee, one of his associates, should be his successor. Lee had served Grace for about twenty years and had demonstrated growth in his leadership skills. He also had the confidence of the people. Lim prayed over

---

[25] Ibid., 30.

this for two years and then began discussing it with his board, and they affirmed Lim's choice. (Grace's constitution requires no congregational vote to implement this transition. The Senior Pastor and Executive church Board are authorized to implement it.)

Lim waited another eighteen months before informing Grace's multiple congregations. Meanwhile, he invited Wayde Goodall, a well-known pastor from the United States, as a third party consultant, to counsel him and Lee about the transition. Goodall advised them about potential problems, but he also strongly encouraged the process.

In May of 2011, Lim formally announced the designation of Calvin Lee as Senior Pastor, effective January 1, 2012. The months between announcement and implementation gave the congregation ample time to adjust to the change before it took place and while Lim was still in leadership.[26]

---

[26] Email interview with David Lim, November 11, 2011.

After the transfer of leadership, Lim's title changed to "Pastor-Mentor." In this role, Lim has a continuing presence in the pulpit. Since Grace Assembly has multiple congregations, preaching is a demanding responsibility, and Lee welcomes Lim's help in this area. However, Lee is the undisputed leader of the church. Lim says, "I will not sit on the church board nor on the leadership team, except by invitation of the Senior Pastor."[27] The strength of the relationship between these two men is further evident in Lim's comment about Lee: "He is his own man and will do things differently from me. My concern is for the future good of the church. I will still remain in the Pastor-Mentor role in the foreseeable future before retirement. He wants me to stay on indefinitely. I want to see him succeed."[28]

Although the benefits of the Asian model are readily apparent, it begs the question: "Can this work with congregational governance?" Keep reading!

---

[27] Ibid.

[28] Ibid.

3

What about Congregational Governance?

"After the eldership confirms it, the congregation should be given the opportunity to confirm it. Then they will have a three-fold witness: the pastor's heart, the eldership's heart, and the heart of the congregation."
Frank Damazio

In contrast to the Asian Church, one obstacle American churches may encounter in creating a plan of pastoral succession involves their congregational form of government that requires the vote of the membership. Rick Seaward, of Singapore's Victory Christian Centre, dealt with this matter rather abruptly when he pastored a church in Hawaii. Convinced that God wanted him to turn the church over to a younger associate and move into an apostolic role, yet constrained by church bylaws requiring a vote, he simply announced to his people, "This is the man the Lord wants to succeed me, so you vote for him!"[29] They did.

In most cases, however, such an approach would backfire. With congregations accustomed to choosing their pastor, the process will necessarily involve more steps. Either the church must change its bylaws, allowing the lead pastor to appoint his successor, or the lead pastor must help the members understand and embrace the transition process through their vote. Of the two options, the latter seems best. In either case, the veteran pastor should initiate the process. According to Bob Russell, author of *Transition Plan*, "A smooth transition must emanate from the preacher and not the [congregation], otherwise the transition is

---

[29] Rick Seaward, Lecture at Victory Family Centre for the course "Apostolic Leadership in Asian Churches" (class notes for D. Min. course, Assemblies of God Theological Seminary, Extension Class, Singapore, October, 2011), 9.

on precarious ground. It's wise for the preacher to suggest the successor, the strategy, the departure date, and his intention afterward."[30]

This makes abundant sense. After all, why should the pastor *not* demonstrate leadership in *this* arena, as he has in other matters affecting the well-being of his congregation? And why not initiate the process while he is still viable, before waning energy and loss of creativity curtail his effectiveness and leave his congregation wondering about the future of their church? Russell adds, "A wise person faces his mortality and a loving person thinks of the next generation. To fail to do both is folly and selfish."[31]

"Trickle Down Communication"

Once the veteran pastor has identified a potential successor, he must carefully lay the groundwork to prepare the congregation. This might include months of pre-announcement teaching, using scriptural

---

[30] Russell and Bucher, *Transition Plan*, 63.

[31] Ibid., 42.

examples of succession. The teaching should carefully explain the rationale for and benefits of a continuity of vision under a new leader who will be mentored by the veteran leader. Of course this assumes that the pastor has already confided the idea to the church board and secured their support (a protracted process in itself, which I will discuss later).

At some point, the pastor should also conduct focus group meetings with various congregational leaders (church staff, ministry leaders, and other volunteers) to explain the concept and hear their feedback. Finally, the concept should be taken to the membership for their vote and then carefully explained from the pulpit to the entire congregation. J. Don George calls this process of informing smaller groups first the "trickle down method of communication."[32]

---

[32] George, *Against the Wind*, Kindle e–book, Location 1031.

First Assembly
Sumter, South Carolina

Pastor Phil Simun followed a similar pattern at First Assembly in Sumter, South Carolina. Having served this church for 38 years as lead pastor, Phil and his wife Linda had been praying about their retirement for two years. Their younger associate, Jason Banar, on staff for 10 years as NextGen pastor, was beginning to sense a call to serve in a lead role— somewhere. During their years of serving together, Phil and Jason had developed a close working relationship. Phil says, "He was like my son. ... I think long-term work together is one key to finding a successor who can successfully take the leadership and go with it."[33] Phil also knew that Jason was well loved and respected by the congregation.

In January of 2013, Phil prepared a "Step-Down Transition Plan" consisting of five major steps that would prepare Jason and the congregation for his transition to lead pastor. Phil began sharing the plan

---

[33] Interview with Phil Simun, January 23, 2015 at First Assembly of God, Sumter, SC and Phil Simun's "Timeline of Transition Events," received by email on February 4, 2015.

with individual board members and other key leaders on a one-to-one basis. Then, in a meeting of the Official Board, he asked them to approve the plan by their vote, which they did. Phil says, "I think giving each of them time to process the news before having the formal meeting was one key to acceptance."[34]

Next, Phil and the Board called the church members together for two special business meetings on March 20th and 27th. In the first, Phil presented the transition plan and recommended their consideration of Jason as the next lead pastor of First Assembly. The meeting was conducted in an informal, relaxed manner, allowing ample time for questions and answers. At the conclusion of the meeting, Phil reminded the people about the next meeting, a week later, when they would be asked to vote.

In the second business meeting, the Official Board nominated Jason to become the next lead pastor at the time of Phil's retirement later that year. (No specific

---

[34] Phil Simun's "Timeline of Transition Events."

date was announced for that.) Jason was elected with 97.5% of the vote.

Over the next five months, Jason assumed an increasing burden of responsibility under Phil's supervision. Not only did he preach more, he also met with the board, made administrative decisions, and began the search for a new youth pastor. During that time, Phil remained in the lead role, but devoted most of his time to mentoring Jason for his new role. On August 25, 2013, Phil preached his final sermon as Lead Pastor of First Assembly, after which the congregation gave him and Linda a retirement celebration.

"Don't Come to Me with Complaints!"

Predictably, the transition has worked well, so well in fact, that Phil is not aware of anyone who left the church because of the pastoral change. He and Linda remain involved in the church, volunteering as the "Senior Saints" Pastor and doing some hospital visitation. He and Jason continue to enjoy a close friendship that includes mutual encouragement and on-going mentoring. Phil says he has not received one complaint from the congregation about Jason. That may be due in part to his admonition to them on the night they elected Jason: "I encourage you to vote for Jason as your next pastor. He has wonderful qualities and I believe he will make a good pastor. However, like all of us, he has faults, and if you vote him in as your pastor, some of those faults will come to light from time to time. When they do, don't come to me with complaints about him. I will not listen." Phil adds, "And the people knew I meant it!"[35]

As in the case of Naomi Dowdy, Phil's transition from lead pastor has freed him for a wider ministry. As a presbyter with the Assemblies of God, he provides encouragement, counsel, and support to other pastors and churches in the Sumter area and beyond.

"A Three-fold Witness"

Even when a church's bylaws don't require the vote of the members, it may be wise to ask the

---

[35] Interview with Phil Simun, January 23, 2015 at First Assembly of God, Sumter, SC

congregation to affirm the transition plan. Frank Damazio offers excellent advice in this regard. Hand-picked by Dick Iverson to fill his shoes as lead pastor at City Bible Church in Portland, Oregon, Damazio commits an entire chapter of his book *The Vanguard Leader* to this subject. Titled, "The Legacy: Passing the Baton," the chapter is a treasure trove of valuable information for churches seeking a plan of succession. Damazio counsels, "The senior pastor must accept the responsibility to raise a successor, and the eldership must understand and support the process."[36] He adds, "After the eldership confirms it, the congregation should be given the opportunity to confirm it. Then they will have a three-fold witness: the pastor's heart, the eldership's heart, and the heart of the congregation."[37] Damazio warns, "Disagreement over a biblical, orderly succession … stirs up dissension that leads to regrettable mistakes with painful consequences."[38]

---

[36] Frank Damazio, *The Vanguard Leader: A New Breed of Leader to Encounter the Future* (Portland, OR: Bible Temple Publishing, 1994), 309.

[37] Ibid., 290.

[38] Ibid., 309.

The good news for any church seeking a pastoral succession plan is that they don't have to go through painful contortions to fit into only one model. If the senior pastor and other key leaders prayerfully seek the wisdom of God, while researching various models and engaging in honest dialogue, the Lord will help them find a plan that works for them. The important thing is to be intentional about developing a process before crisis demands it.

In the next chapter we will look at a couple of other models, including the recent transfer of leadership from Tommy Barnett to his son Luke at Phoenix First Assembly. We'll also note some important similarities between relay races and pastoral succession and a concept known as "overlap timing."

4

No
One-Size-Fits-All
Model

"If the exchange is handled properly,
it's possible to gain a step during the transition."
Bob Russell

Pastor Bob Russell led Southeast Christian Church in Louisville, Kentucky through a successful pastoral transition that began in 1999. (He tells the full story in his book *Transition Plan.*) That year the church moved into a brand new 70 million dollar facility with a 9,000-seat sanctuary.

At age 56, Russell had been their pastor for 34 years. Although he felt "vibrant and excited about the future," he began to pray and talk with his board about a successor.[39] Their minds turned to their associate pastor, Dave Stone. Sixteen years younger than Russell, Stone had been on staff for 10 years, and was "highly regarded and loved—especially by the younger members of the church." The transition plan called for Stone, who was already sharing the preaching schedule, to preach more. Gradually, over a seven year time frame, he would preach a little more and Russell would preach a little less. At some point after six years, Stone would assume the role of lead pastor. Russell announced the plan to the congregation in October of 1999, and Dave Stone became Senior Minister in January of 2006. At that point Russell remained on staff for a period of time as an "adviser" and continued to participate in the preaching schedule.

---

[39] Russell and Bucher, *Transition Plan*, 15.

Pastoral Transition and Relay Races

Like Frank Damazio, Bob Russell compares a good pastoral transition to a relay race.[40] He says that one benefit of this kind of race is that multiple runners can cover the distance faster than a single runner. The most crucial moment in a relay race is the passing of the baton, and relay teams practice it for hours.

Russell offers several observations about the transfer, each highly suggestive of pastoral transition: 1) The one passing the baton must keep running at full steam until the baton is passed. 2) The one receiving the baton must start running before he receives it. 3) Both runners must remain in the same lane. 4) The baton must be passed in a timely manner. 5) After the exchange, the one passing the baton leaves the race to cheer for his successor.

Russell mentions one other benefit of the relay: "If the exchange is handled properly, it's possible to gain a step during the transition."[41] This "extra step"

---

[40] Ibid., 46.

[41] Ibid., 47.

serves as a metaphor of the dynamic thrust that occurs when veteran and successor collaborate on mission, strategies, and tactics. Each brings a unique perspective to the process that cross-pollinates and produces a more powerful composite. The wise man Solomon said it well: "Two are better than one, because they have a good return for their work" (Eccl. 4:9).

Russell recommends that upon full retirement, the veteran pastor step out of ministry altogether in that church. He followed his own advice, choosing not to return to his church for a full year after his retirement, and then, only as a member with no pastoral role. He saw this as the best way to give Stone a wide berth to develop his own leadership patterns. In fact, Russell strongly advises that when the transition is complete, the veteran leader resolutely refuse any ministry role in that church, present or future.

On the other hand, some transition models encourage a continuing role for the veteran, such as Lim's "Pastor-Mentor" model (cited in chapter two). A similar case is that of Pastor Tommy Barnett, founder of the Los Angeles Dream Center, who for many years also led the renowned First Assembly of God in Phoenix, Arizona.

Tommy and Luke Barnett

In the fall of 2013, Tommy Barnett concluded his legendary role as senior pastor of Phoenix First Assembly. His son Luke succeeded him. "I probably never would have stepped down," says Tommy, "because it was my plan to lead until I died. But God knew it was the best thing. He had to slow me down to put the man in there that he needed."[42] Tommy explains that two unforeseen events led to the leadership transition: A crisis in his health and Luke's unexpected reappearance at First Assembly.

Following a successful pastorate in Whittier, California, Luke Barnett surprised his dad by moving back to Phoenix and serving as a volunteer in First Assembly, his home church. Observing Luke's diligence and faithfulness, the church board

---

[42] Interview with Tommy Barnett, April 30, 2015.

encouraged Tommy to hire him for a staff position, which he did.

A few years later, when Tommy's heart valve surgery required a three-month recovery, he asked Luke to lead the church during his absence. Under Luke's leadership, the church grew faster than before. People kept telling Tommy, "The church is doing well—even better!"

When Tommy returned to the pulpit, he announced to his congregation that, going forward, Luke would serve as "Lead Pastor," and Tommy would continue in the role of "Senior Pastor." This intermediate phase of leadership gave Luke increased authority and responsibility, while the church remained under Tommy's superintending hand.

A similar pattern can be seen in the case of Moses and Joshua. According to Deuteronomy 31, Joshua did not assume full leadership of Israel until Moses was about to die. However, at some point well in advance of that, God instructed Moses to bring Joshua before the people, lay his hands on him, and "transfer *some of* your authority to him so the whole community will obey him" (Num. 27:20 NLT, emphasis mine). Although Joshua had been Moses' loyal assistant for nearly forty years, this "pre-commissioning" ceremony elevated Joshua to a higher level of authority in the eyes of the people while Moses was still their official leader. It also gave Joshua the opportunity to try his hand at decision-making while still under Moses' watchful eye (see Numbers 27:21). The benefits of such an intermediate phase are obvious.

In the case of the Barnetts, the intermediate phase lasted about three years. Then, Tommy determined it was time for Luke to assume the role of Senior Pastor. He spoke with his board about it, and they agreed. In fact, they told him they didn't want to consider any other candidate. In a Sunday morning worship service, Tommy presented the idea to the congregation, and took a vote. They unanimously called Luke to become their new Senior Pastor.[43]

---

[43] First Assembly had recently changed its bylaws regarding church membership, which is now comprised of everyone who regularly attends the church.

A New Dream

Ironically, Tommy's ultimate decision to step aside was not due to failing health. After his recovery from heart surgery, he experienced renewed energy and vigor, and, concerning pastoral leadership, he thought to himself, "I can still do this!" Nevertheless, he knew the transition to Luke's leadership was best for the church.

But, what was he to do with all his new-found energy and drive? Tommy says, "I had to get a new dream. I don't think you should ever catch up with your dream. So my new dream is to help others fulfill their dreams. I do conferences—one almost every week. I did ten overseas last year."[44] Tommy's experience confirms Dowdy's premise that leadership transition is not a dead end for seasoned leadership, but an opportunity to move on "from succession to [greater] significance."

---

[44] Interview with Tommy Barnett, April 30, 2015.

A Continuing Role for the Veteran

Although his new dream requires extensive travel, Tommy remains involved at First Assembly, where he is referred to as "Co-Pastor." He preaches about once every six weeks, which suits him just fine.[45] His preference is to sit on the front row on Sundays and cheer for Luke. Tommy also spends several hours each day in the church office. However, Luke makes all decisions affecting the church, and Tommy carefully avoids interfering. "I only give advice if they ask for it. If you're always pushing advice, they'll run from it."[46]

Tommy's continuing role with First Assembly allows him to use his considerable influence to support the new senior pastor. He tells of an older, wealthy couple who were major donors to the church. When they learned of the coming leadership change, they told Tommy they would be leaving First Assembly.

---

[45] Tommy says preaching has never been his favorite part of ministry. "I like building things and creating programs and ministries. To me, preaching is not a masterpiece that you present. It's an old greasy wrench you fix things with."

[46] Interview with Tommy Barnett, April 30, 2015.

However, out of respect for Tommy, they agreed to give Luke three Sundays, then make their decision. They chose to remain with the church, confiding to Tommy, "Luke is a better preacher than you!" Tommy observes, "It has been proven; the new paradigm is: the churches that succeed are churches where the [veteran] pastor, who has had a long and effective ministry, stayed on and affirmed the new pastor."[47]

"Overlap Timing"

With all the benefits that come with keeping the veteran involved at the church, it also presents challenges that should not be ignored. Weese and Crabtree call this arrangement "overlap timing," and observe that "of all the options, … overlap timing is the most emotionally and spiritually challenging."[48] To be sure, overlap timing can only work when a high level of trust exists between the veteran and

---

[47] Ibid.

[48] Weese and Crabtree, *The Elephant in the Boardroom*, Kindle e–book, Location 834.

successor, and both they and their spouses are prepared to embrace its challenges.

Even then, because of human weakness and the potential for misunderstanding, the transition should be clearly defined and include specific phases and dates for completion, along with role expectations. A third party consultant, trusted by both veteran and successor, can assist them in this process, something Weese and Crabtree highly recommend.[49] The particulars of the transition should be stated in a memorandum of understanding, adopted by the official board, and signed by both pastors.

Even though there is no "one-size-fits-all" model, every succession plan should include these and a few other critically important components to help avoid the kind of failure that occurred at Dallas First Baptist. But, that is a subject for the next chapter.

---

[49] Ibid., Kindle e–book, Location 1525.

5

Components of a Successful Plan

"Obscured in all of this was the one pivotal question: How long would Criswell remain with his title, in his office, preaching at the church? This was the paramount question that should have been officially addressed. It would have saved the church … enormous heartache and a historical (sic) crisis."
Dr. Joel Gregory

At the end of the previous chapter, I observed that a successful transition plan will include several crucial components including specific phases with dates for completion and role expectations, among other things. These should be spelled out in a memorandum of understanding, adopted by the church board, and signed by the veteran and successor. At appropriate times, the plan should also be clearly communicated to the congregation. The absence of these specific components accounts for transition failures like the one that occurred at the prominent, 29,000-member First Baptist Church of Dallas, Texas.

A Plan that Failed

In November 1990, at the invitation of Pastor W.A. Criswell and his board, Dr. Joel Gregory joined the staff as Criswell's chosen successor. The plan would make Gregory the third pastor of First Baptist in a hundred years—a point of pride for this historic church. However, on Sept 30, 1992, less than two years into the process, Gregory abruptly resigned.

In his book, *Too Great a Temptation: The Seductive Power of America's Super Church,* Gregory explains the reason for his resignation. The transition plan involved no specific dates as to when the actual transfer of leadership would happen. This vagueness provided a breeding ground for frustration. Criswell's reluctance to step down and Gregory's eagerness to take the reins were compounded by confusion and conflicting loyalties in the congregation. Unable or unwilling to manage the ensuing frustration, Gregory left.

Recalling the interview process that led to the plan, Gregory laments: "Obscured in all of this was the one pivotal question: How long would Criswell remain with his title, in his office, preaching at the church? This was the paramount question that should have been officially addressed. It would have saved the church, the Criswells, and the Gregorys enormous heartache and a historical (*sic*) crisis."[50]

This recalls an important factor in Russell's analogy of the relay race. He says there are two distinct lines on the track, and the transfer must occur between them.[51] Similarly, pastoral transition cannot be extended indefinitely. Russell adds, "Just as locks keep honest people honest, a good transition plan

---

[50] Joel Gregory, *Too Great a Temptation: The Seductive Power of America's Super Church* (Ft. Worth, TX: The Summit Group, 1994), 144.

[51] Russell and Bucher, *Transition Plan*, 46.

with clear lines of authority and a definite time frame helps avoid conflict and uncertainty."[52]

Other Problems to Watch

David Lim, of Singapore's Grace Assembly, cautions about other potential problems with succession plans. He says they will fail if the leaders: 1) Have not clearly understood and upheld the authority of the new leader. 2) Have not respected the veteran leader, recognizing the value of his experience and wisdom as an ongoing contribution to the new leader and the congregation. 3) Have not considered the congregation's perception of the relational interplay between the veteran leader and the new leader. 4) Have not considered the financial needs of the outgoing veteran leader. 5) Have not been mutually respectful.[53]

---

[52] Ibid., 60.

[53] Email interview with David Lim, November 11, 2011.

Nuts and Bolts of a Successful Plan

In addition to clearly defined phases with specific dates well communicated to the congregation, a good transition plan will include several other components.

Financial Considerations

First, there should be some kind of financial consideration for the veteran pastor. The nature of that consideration will depend on the circumstances of the transition and the church's financial ability. In some cases it may simply involve a generous, one-time gift. In others, it may involve continuing income after the transfer, especially if the veteran has a long history with the church, has been instrumental in the church's success, or will remain on the pastoral staff. For example, Tommy Barnett receives a salary for his continuing role at Phoenix First Assembly, but less than he made as senior pastor.[54]

---

[54] Interview with Tommy Barnett, April 30, 2015. (Although the board wanted to continue paying him at his previous level, Tommy declined the full amount because of his diminished responsibilities with the church.)

When the veteran retires from the staff, financial consideration is also in order.[55] Bob Russell, former pastor of Southeast Community Church, is a case in point. Now in retirement, he continues to receive income from the church he served for more than 30 years. In his book, *Transition Plan*, Russell includes the statement drafted by his official board at the time of his retirement outlining the reasons why churches should provide income to long-term pastors in their retirement years. The statement points out that pastors typically earn far less than other professionals, and therefore, they do not have discretionary funds for a retirement plan.[56]

Obviously, smaller churches will not be able to match what larger churches do for their veteran pastors, but every church can do something. The process of determining the amount will be a balancing act between the veteran's need and the church's ability. It should take into consideration the church's size and

---

[55] For a biblical precedent for retirement from ministerial duties, see Numbers 8:23-26.

[56] Russell and Bucher, *Transition Plan*, 63-64.

financial strength, so it doesn't cripple the church's ability to hire other staff and carry on viable ministry. Any veteran pastor who loves the church would certainly not want that. As always, he will continue seeking the church's well-being above his own.

On the other hand, the church should not excuse itself from a financial commitment because it doesn't see currently available cash flow for it. God honors faith and will provide for worthy ventures undertaken in faith. At the church I serve, every time we have initiated a building program or hired new staff or launched a major outreach, we have done it by faith. The money was not apparent in the moment, but God honored our faith and provided as we moved forward. Similarly, when a church commits to trust God and honor their veteran leader in a tangible way, God will honor the church and bless its finances.

There is a sense in which the church helps itself when it helps its veteran leader. Fear of facing financial shortfall might tempt a pastor to stay in the lead role too long. When the church offers to financially assist the pastor in his retirement, it not only honors and cares for God's servant, it also benefits the congregation by hastening the transfer of leadership.

The veteran, successor, and church leadership should pray and work together to determine a reasonable retirement plan. In so doing, they create a culture of mutual honor that pays back huge dividends to all concerned. They also leave a testimony of God's gracious generosity at work in His church.

Commissioning Service

Another component of a good transition plan is a public commissioning service that celebrates both the veteran and successor. As we noted in the previous chapter, God instructed Moses to have Joshua "stand before Eleazar the priest *and the entire assembly and commission him in their presence* ... so the whole Israelite community will obey him" (Num. 27:18-20 emphasis added).

Bob Russell recommends the use of symbols that visually convey the transfer of leadership. He cites the example of Jim Henry, Senior Pastor of First Baptist Church in Orlando, Florida, who washed the feet of his successor before the entire congregation—a powerful expression of servant leadership. Russell, on the other hand, chose to use a baton in commissioning his successor. As he handed it to him in the sight of the congregation, he challenged him to continue the race with diligence.[57] "The symbol tells a story in ways words aren't able to accomplish. They stick in people's minds, embodying the values and priorities. ... Symbols communicate a lot and can serve as a future reminder of what's important."[58]

At some point in the commissioning service, the congregation should be given opportunity to express their support for the new leader, perhaps by a standing ovation. After Joshua's installation as Moses' successor, the elders of Israel declared to him: "Whatever you have commanded us we will do, and wherever you send us we will go. Just as we fully obeyed Moses, so we will obey you. Only may the

---

[57] Ibid., 79.

[58] Ibid.

Lord your God be with you as he was with Moses"
(Josh. 1:16-18).

Holy Spirit Confirmation

Tommy Barnett also chose to use a baton in
commissioning his son Luke, but an unplanned
incident did even more to confirm divine favor on the
event. During the commissioning service, Tommy
asked the members of the church board to join him
and Luke on the stage. At a particular moment in the
proceedings, one of the board members, a medical
doctor, gave a message in tongues. In the
interpretation that followed, the board member said,
"This is God's man. This is God's will. The church
will go forward greater than ever before."[59]

Tommy recalls that twenty-one years before, when he
presented the vision for the Dream Center to his
congregation, the same board member brought a
similarly encouraging prophetic utterance. Without a
doubt, the combination of symbolic imagery and

---

[59] This is Tommy's paraphrase of the actual interpretation as
he recalled it during my interview with him on April 30, 2015.

prophetic gifts greatly encouraged the congregation and helped launch the successful leadership transition at Phoenix First Assembly.

Continuing Relationship

Third, following the transfer, the veteran and successor should maintain a relationship of genuine affection and mutual respect, observable to the congregation. Bob Russell and David Lim underscore the value of ongoing fellowship between veteran and successor, involving mentoring and encouragement. The veteran has a huge opportunity—and responsibility—to help the new leader succeed by strongly supporting and celebrating him to the members of the congregation. This should happen in public settings and private conversations. A wise veteran will never criticize his successor. More than that, the veteran should patently refuse to hear criticism about the successor. At the same time, a wise successor will honor his predecessor. "People's antennas are up in a time of transition and the new leader needs to convince the flock that he honors the past while still focusing on the future."[60]

These relational standards also apply to the spouses of the two leaders. They can contribute greatly to the peaceful transfer of leadership and the success of the successor. On the other hand, a pastor's spouse can sabotage the transition by careless words and unchecked attitudes. This was a factor in the failed transition at Dallas First Baptist, according to Joel Gregory.[61]

~~~~~~~~~~~~~~~~~~~~~

Even with all these components in place, pastoral change—like any major change—will produce some turbulence within the congregation. If properly understood and managed, this turbulence can actually work for the good of the church, as we shall see in the next chapter.

---

[60] Russell and Bucher, *Transition Plan*, 72.

[61] Joel Gregory, *Too Great a Temptation*, 305.

6

Manage the Turbulence

"The greatest resistance to change occurs when a
church is at its peak—precisely the point when
change is needed the most."
Kevin G. Ford

On October 14, 1947, Air Force test pilot
Chuck Yaeger climbed into the cockpit of the rocket-
powered Bell X-1 aircraft. That day he would make
history. He would be the first person to fly faster than
the speed of sound. At an altitude of 45,000 feet, he
would exceed Mach 1 and "break the sound barrier."

The test flight was considered so dangerous that
Yaeger's friends whispered their hopes that his life
insurance was paid up. To complicate matters, two
days before the scheduled flight, Yaeger broke two

ribs in a horseback riding accident. Afraid his injuries, if known, might disqualify him from the test, he sought treatment from a veterinarian in a nearby town. By flight time his pain was so severe he couldn't close the hatch over the cockpit, so a friend rigged a piece of broom handle, providing the needed leverage.

One account of the flight says that as Yaeger approached Mach 1, the aircraft encountered severe turbulence and began to vibrate almost uncontrollably—a situation that didn't help his pain. Of greater concern was his fear that the aircraft could not withstand such violent forces. Yaeger was tempted to pull back on the throttle. Instead, he defied his fear and pushed the throttle forward. As he broke the sound barrier, the turbulence ceased and the flight became perfectly smooth.

"Disequilibrium"

This story provides an apt analogy of what often happens when a church plans and implements major change. It encounters turbulence. In organizational theory, the term for this turbulence is "disequilibrium." The word refers to the unsettling effects major change produces in people. It affects their emotions and manifests in their attitudes, words, and behavior. It can translate into nervous excitement, uncertainty, tension, anger, or fear. Sometimes it results in disgruntled members resisting the change or leaving the church.

The Rock of Wilmington

In 1988, Ron and Norma McGee moved to Wilmington, North Carolina to plant The Rock, an inter-denominational charismatic church. Three years later, their 18-year-old son, Bryan, came on staff as the janitor. Over the years, as Bryan matured, he assumed various ministry roles including youth and children's director, small groups coordinator, and ultimately, associate pastor.

As the church approached its 20th anniversary, a series of events brought Ron face to face with the church's need for a new leader. For some time, his health had been declining, affecting his physical stamina and cognitive skills. His family called for a "sit down" consultation with him. Concerned for his survival, they encouraged him to pull back from some of his pastoral responsibilities.

Wrestling in prayer over the situation, Ron received a word from the Lord: "If you are going to reach a 21st century generation, you need a 21st century leader who shares your vision and can advance the church on its mission."[62] His mind turned immediately to Bryan, who by that time had been on staff for 17 years, serving in virtually every role in the church. Bryan was 35 years old, highly experienced in ministry, and loved by the congregation. And he loved them—a fact proven by his years of devoted service.

Once sure of his direction, Ron presented the idea of leadership transition to his "presbytery"—the church's governing board consisting of the pastoral staff and three non-resident elders (also pastors). They confirmed the idea and Ron began preparing the congregation by teaching frequently on the subject

---

[62] Interview with Ron and Norma McGee, February 6, 2015.

and talking to various key leaders. The plan called for Ron to remain on staff in a salaried position as "Founding Pastor," but with fewer responsibilities. He would oversee small groups, teach a foundations class for new members, and lead the pastoral care ministry. Bryan would assume the role of Senior Pastor with ultimate decision-making authority. Ron says, "We just changed seats on the bus. He had worked for me for seventeen years. Now, I worked for him."

They planned for the transition to take effect in 2008 at the church's 20th anniversary celebration, which they announced to the congregation three months ahead of the event. (Their governing structure required no vote from the congregation.) The fact that Ron would remain involved with the church comforted long-time members and helped ease the transition. Norma recalls, "The congregation so respected the depth of Ron's experience and knowledge, that his continuing role in the life of the church reassured them."

As further assurance to the people, Ron also retained

a limited presence in the pulpit. Prior to the transition, he preached 70 percent of the time. After the transition he preached 40 percent of the time and later, 20 percent. Three years after the transition went into effect, Ron "retired" from his official duties with the church. He continues to teach a class and do some limited hospital visitation, and he and Norma attend the annual staff retreat. As appreciation for his founding role and many years of service, the church pays him a small retirement income.

Turbulence Is Unavoidable

Even with all of this preparation, The Rock encountered disequilibrium. A number of people left the church. Ron remembers, "We lost people because I wasn't doing all the preaching. Some of the older people simply preferred my preaching to Bryan's." Nevertheless, Ron and the staff endured the turbulence and forged ahead with the transition.

In the midst of turbulence, leaders face the powerful temptation to retreat from the proposed change. Like Chuck Yaeger in the X-1, pastors fear the whole thing will come apart and disintegrate into a thousand pieces. Failure to understand the unavoidable nature of disequilibrium can result in decisions that hurt the church more than help. For example, leaders err when they assume that turning back is a solution—or even possible. Although turning back *may* satisfy those who oppose the change (or it may not), it will aggravate and unsettle others who favor it. Either way (going forward or turning back) will involve turbulence.

Once the new normal has been announced, once the change is underway, there is no going back to the old normal. The best thing leaders can do when encountering the turbulence of change is to pray for the sustaining grace of God (and nerves of steel!) to follow through. Like Yaeger, they must keep pushing forward on the throttle, and like him, they will ultimately break through to tranquility. All the while, they must remain positive in faith, gracious toward the opposition, and reassuring to the committed.

That's what happened at The Rock. Although some people left because they preferred Ron's preaching, in the years since, there has been a positive shift toward

Bryan. Ron says, "Now, we have younger people in our congregation who prefer Bryan's preaching to mine." Ron and Norma are convinced that, despite the challenges, the transition was right for the church, for them, and for Bryan. Their relationship with Bryan has never been better. Ron observes, "It's been six years, and there's never been a cross word between us." Norma says, "For years, Ron told our people that he was laying a foundation that the next generation would build on. Bryan often refers to that statement from the pulpit, and he frequently shares lessons he learned from his dad."

Leaders must let go of the unrealistic idea that if they do everything right, they will avoid turbulence. The simple fact is, turbulence is rarely avoidable. To press forward in spite of turbulence seems to contradict all logic, yet it is usually the prudent course of action. Following are a few other facts about change and disequilibrium that are counterintuitive. Understanding these paradoxes will strengthen the leader's resolve in the face of turbulence.

Turbulence Is Healthy

Not only is disequilibrium unavoidable if the church is to move forward, a certain amount of it is healthy. Even before the change has a chance to demonstrate its benefits, the commotion associated with it is enough to shake people awake and dislodge organizational inertia. Disequilibrium in appropriate doses can pull the church out of complacency and stagnation and stimulate new growth. This is necessary from time to time, because churches, like other organizations, can slip into decline, particularly as they approach maturity.

Dr. Ichak Adizes, an expert in organizational health, says, "Organizations have lifecycles just as living organisms do."[63] What is true of other organizations, is true of local churches: They also go through the stages of a life cycle. These stages include birth, childhood, adolescence, maturity, and—without strategic changes at critical moments—decline and even death.

---

[63] Ichak Adizes, *Corporate Lifecycles: How and Why Corporations Grow and Die and What To Do About It,* (Englewood Cliffs, New Jersey: Prentice Hall, 1988), xiii.

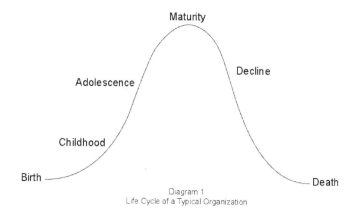

Diagram 1
Life Cycle of a Typical Organization

If one imagines a bell-shaped curve, the birth of the church is represented at the bottom left and the maturity stage is at the top of the bell (see diagram 1). As it grows through childhood and adolescence, church life is characterized by excitement, messiness, and a lot of uncertainty. It involves a constant, arduous climb, always pressing, always reaching for another level, always unsure if the effort will pay off. Aggressive outreach is essential to its very survival. Change is the one constant.

Arriving at maturity, however, it begins to enjoy a measure of stability and predictability. Attendance-wise, it has achieved "critical mass," and financially, revenues seem adequate. Programs, buildings, and other infrastructure have become its priority. Aggressive outreach seems less essential. The church turns inward in focus, unaware that it is resting on its laurels—and on this nice, comfortable plateau called "maturity."

For individual people, maturity is the ideal. For organizations, maturity is the danger zone. Unless something happens to alter its course, the next phase is decline, which is followed by death. Organizations, including churches, can and do die. They die because they become comfortable, then complacent, then stagnant. They die because, as Thom Rainer puts it in *Autopsy of a Deceased Church*, they no longer have a vision.[64] To avoid decline and death, churches must experience strategic change, and strategic change produces healthy disequilibrium.

Success Resists Change

Oddly enough, a church's success actually breeds resistance to change. After all, when things are going

---

[64] Thom S. Rainer, *Autopsy of a Dead Church: 12 Ways to Keep Yours Alive*, (B&H Publishing Group: Nashville, TN, 2014), Kindle e-book, Location 61.

well, why change? Yet, that is when the need for change is most urgent. According to Kevin G. Ford, "The greatest resistance to change occurs when a church is at its peak—precisely the point when change is needed the most."[65]

Ford cites the work of Charles Handy, a British business writer, who uses what he calls the "Sigmoid Curve" or "S Curve" graphic to illustrate the normal life cycle of an organization. Imagine again the bell-shaped curve with the word "maturity" at the top. As the church grows toward that point, it follows a trajectory similar in shape to an S curve. At the end of the S curve, is a plateau, followed by a steep descent—the other side of the bell curve. In order to avoid plateauing and decline, Handy says an organization needs a new challenge or vision—a new "S Curve"—complete with the uncertainty, messiness, and excitement that characterized the church's childhood and adolescence. In other words, the church must be willing to forego the seeming

---

[65] Kevin G. Ford, *Transforming Church: Bringing Out the Good to Get to Great*, (Tyndale House Publishers, Inc., 2007) 161-162.

benefits of maturity—comfort, predictability, and smug complacency—and take new risks (see diagram 2). Ford refers to this kind of change as "transformational change."[66]

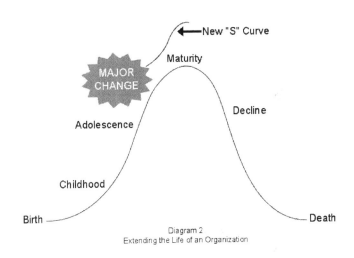

Diagram 2
Extending the Life of an Organization

Change or Die

Let me hasten to add that a true church is more than an organization; it is a living *organism* pulsating with the life of God. Perhaps Adizes' and Hardy's organizational concepts cannot be applied to a church in an absolute sense. To be sure, churches alive with

---

[66] Ibid.

the power of the Holy Spirit will *not* decline and die.

Nevertheless, human nature remains the same whether in a secular organization or in a church. Left to themselves, people often grow complacent and spiritually stagnant. That is why Jesus gave pastors as gifts to the church to keep it moving forward (Eph. 4:11,12). That is why the Holy Spirit continually leads pastors to inspire new vision in their people and offer fresh challenges to their congregations—hence, transformational change. Don George says, "There are only two kinds of churches in America—changing churches and dying churches. A church that's not changing is dying."[67]

Nevertheless, the key to avoiding decline in the church is not to arbitrarily change leaders, nor to brainstorm for some novel scheme that might generate excitement—some new "S Curve." The key is for leaders to follow the Holy Spirit, just as Moses and the Israelites followed the Cloud in the wilderness. In that experience, change was the one

---

[67] Don George said this in a sermon at the South Carolina Assemblies of God District Council in May, 2014.

constant. Stagnation occurred only when they stopped following, such as at Kadesh-Barnea (Num. 13:26-33). Because the Holy Spirit is the ever-creative, renewing Presence within the Church, a truly Spirit-led church will not stagnate. But, it must change!

New Leadership is Not Enough

I am not advocating arbitrary change for the sake of change, and I'm certainly not saying that just changing leadership will result in new vitality for the church. In fact, a common misconception in the arena of corporate business is that simply changing CEOs will renew the company. Assuming that, corporations rotate CEOs, football teams rotate coaches, and some churches rotate pastors.

However, Adizes argues that "changing the rider won't make a mule into a race horse."[68] An organization in decline has systemic problems—problems in its very DNA—that will not go away just because a new leader takes over. Adizes uses another analogy about an old truck that has broken down and

---

[68] Adizes, *Corporate Lifecycles,* 100.

stopped on the road. Changing drivers will not necessarily fix the truck.

Applying this to pastoral transition, the new leader, at the appropriate time, will need to implement bold, systemic changes. Hence, the congregation should not be led to believe that after the transition, all will be as before. They should be prepared that the new leader will be different from the previous leader, even though he shares the same vision. They should be told that at some point, the new leader will call for strategic changes—changes that are essential to the viability of the church. Of course, as we learned in chapter one, the best scenario is achieved when some of those needed changes are well underway before the pastoral transition is even announced, as in the case of Don George and Ben Dailey at Calvary Church.

Having established the positive benefits of transformational change, a cautionary word is in order…

Too Much Turbulence Can Crash the Plane!

Too much disequilibrium at one time can harm the organization. Applied to pastoral transition, this means that the new leader, while knowing more changes are needed, must go slow in implementing them.

A change in pastoral leadership is huge. In fact, few if any changes a church ever goes through will equal it in intensity. To compound that change with other major changes too quickly is to subject the "aircraft" to impossible pressures (to return to our previous analogy). If Chuck Yaeger, while trying to break the sound barrier, had also tried to set a new altitude record, he might have crashed the plane.

Bob Russell counsels the new leader to practice patience when implementing major changes. "A change of ministers is a huge transition for people and a wise successor needs to ... give the congregation a year or two before implementing dramatic change. That is difficult because the new preacher may be totally convinced that dramatic change is necessary.

… But too much change too fast disorients people and is usually counterproductive."[69]

~~~~~~~~~~~~~~

Hopefully, these facts about organizational health will encourage pastors and churches to overcome their fear of change and move forward in planning for leadership transition. Transformational change should not be feared. With all its uncertainty and messiness, it can create new excitement for the church and new potential for growth.

Under the Spirit's guidance, leaders are change agents. Aware of the potential danger of stagnation and decline, effective leaders will remain flexible and dependent on the Spirit. They will invest the necessary time seeking God, listening for His promptings. They will read, learn, dialogue with their team, and take the risks associated with obedience. They will live close to His heart and remain

---

[69] Russell and Bucher, *Transition Plan*, 68.

vulnerable to hear a "word in season," such as Ron McGee heard at a crucial juncture: "If you are going to reach a 21st century generation, you need a 21st century leader who shares your vision and can advance the church's mission." When leaders hear such a word, they should break camp and follow the Cloud, because the Holy Spirit is about to create His own new "S Curve!"

~~~~~~~~~~~~~~~

By this point in your reading, you may have concluded that planning for pastoral change is an imperative. You may also be wondering about how to take the first step. Thankfully, there's a good answer for that, something our final chapter will explore.

7

Where Do We Begin?

"[Crisis planning] can help get people thinking strategically about a pastoral change and the need to do generic transition planning."
Carolyn Weese and J. Russell Crabtree

An old adage reminds us that "the journey of a thousand miles begins with the first step." Sometimes that first step is the most difficult, particularly if the journey involves uncharted territory and unknown risks. Leadership change is a formidable topic, especially if you're the leader. Especially if you've *been* the leader for a long time and were instrumental in the church's birth, development, or growth. Thinking of someone else as the leader of your church is kind of like choosing your wife's next husband. The truth is, you're not sure anyone can take care of her as well as you. You love this church, you're concerned about it, and that loving concern can be a barrier to transition planning. Recall Tommy Barnett's comment: "It was my plan to lead until I died."[70]

Consider another potential barrier to transition planning—the people you lead, the people of the congregation who love you and don't want to think about any other pastor but you. You've served them for years, maybe decades. You've cried with them in their valleys and rejoiced with them in their victories. You've planned and worked together with them to see the church become what it is today. They won't hear any talk of another leader. The emotional bond that links you is just too strong for such talk.

And yet, at a deeper level, you know it is a necessary conversation. Vitally necessary. You buy life insurance to protect your family when the inevitable occurs. For the same reason, you are going to create a

---

[70] Interview with Tommy Barnett, April 30, 2015.

plan to care for the church when the time comes for new leadership. You have led them in other important ways. You will not shirk this responsibility. You will lead them in transition planning, because that's what responsible leaders do.

The First Step

In their book, *The Elephant in the Boardroom: Speaking the Unspoken about Pastoral Transitions,* Weese and Crabtree acknowledge that talking about pastoral change can be daunting, both for the pastor and the congregation. The subject looms like the proverbial "elephant in the room" that no one wants to confront. As a way to get started—as a "first step" in the journey of transition planning—Weese and Crabtree recommend the development of a Crisis Transition Plan. In their words, such planning can "help get people thinking strategically about a pastoral change and the need to do generic transition planning."[71]

---

[71] Weese and Crabtree, *The Elephant in the Boardroom*, Kindle e-book, Location 1896.

Additionally, they point out that crisis planning is "no-fault"—it does not imply that the pastor is leaving or that the church wants that to happen. It does not assume an immediate change in leadership. Nor does it necessarily involve a known successor. It is simply a prudent response to the *possibility* of the unexpected.

Like everyone else, pastors are subject to circumstances that could abruptly remove them from their role of leadership in the church. No one wants to think about it, but pastors have faced debilitating illness, emotional collapse, marriage or family problems, moral failure, death, or more positively, a call to another ministry. When pastoral change occurs suddenly with no prior planning, churches often find themselves in confusion and dysfunction. To avoid such a scenario, some pastors have found it prudent to lead their churches in planning for the unexpected.

Weese and Crabtree suggest five critical components for a Crisis Transition Plan: Safety, Command Structure, Continuity of Service, Communication, and Restoration of Normalcy. Following is a brief summary of each. However, I recommend that every pastor get their book, which contains far more information about each of these important components.

Safety

This component involves the spiritual and emotional well-being of congregation members who may be in shock or grief at the sudden loss of their pastor. This is particularly needed if the pastor had a long and successful tenure, or if his departure involves a serious crisis. Weese and Crabtree recommend "critical incident debriefing … for the church staff and lay leadership, and perhaps for the entire church."[72] Furthermore, if the pastor was in the process of counseling or assisting certain individuals in the congregation, these should be contacted and offered alternative resources.

---

[72] Ibid., Kindle e-book, Location 1839.

Command Structure

During the emergency phase of the crisis, which can last from 24 hours to a week, collaborative decision making by a board or other group may prove difficult or impossible. For this reason, a good Crisis Transition Plan will designate an acting head of staff and authorize him or her to make decisions during this phase of the crisis. The plan should clearly outline the authority delegated to the acting head of staff and this should be communicated to the board and staff ahead of time to encourage compliance. The plan should also identify a secondary head of staff in case the primary is not available.

Continuity of Service

Because the corporate worship experience is vital to the congregation's sense of well-being, the plan should identify a trusted pastor who would be available to provide effective pulpit ministry in the first few weeks of the crisis. If this pastor is already known to the congregation, he or she will be far more capable of inspiring confidence and promoting healing. The plan should also identify other leaders who can continue in an interim capacity until a new pastor can be secured. Weese and Crabtree refer to these leaders as "bridging resources." These individuals should be contacted in advance to determine their willingness and to negotiate terms of service (compensation, expense reimbursement, etc.).

Other bridging resources might include administrative and financial considerations. For example, the plan should identify files in the church office where information on bank accounts, persons authorized to sign checks, and computer passwords can be found.

Communication

Generally, only one person in the church should handle communication during the crisis, and the plan should specify that person. Early in the crisis, that individual should communicate with all groups who will be affected by the pastoral change: the staff, lay leaders, congregation, area pastors, denominational leaders, friends of the church, and the media. Church staff should be trained in advance about communication in times of crisis, as to what kinds of information they can release and what questions should be referred to the director of communications.

Restoration of Normalcy

At some point following the emergency phase of the crisis, the church can undertake an orderly process to recruit a new pastor. The crisis plan should lay out the steps for that process. Weese and Crabtree offer a number of helpful suggestions for that.[73]

~~~~~~~~~~~~

Once the Crisis Transition Plan has been formulated, copies should be given to all participants as well as to key leaders in the church. Because every congregation experiences changes in lay leadership and staff, the plan should be updated annually.

To summarize, when churches intentionally plan for crisis, they save themselves major upheaval when the unexpected occurs. The best plans are initiated by

---

[73] Ibid., Kindle e–book, Locations 1891–2155.

pastors who wisely face such a possibility and lead their board and congregation in confronting the "elephant." Such plans can become the first step toward a broader, more long-range plan of pastoral succession.

Conclusion

When churches intentionally plan for pastoral transition, they save themselves major upheaval when the inevitable occurs. They also gain substantial benefits including the timely and stable transfer of leadership and the continuity of vision. Like the hand-off of the baton in a relay race, a good transition plan helps the church gain an "extra step" by combining the creative energy of a younger leader with the wisdom of an experienced veteran.[74]

The best plans are initiated by veteran pastors who wisely face their inevitable withdrawal from leadership. Tommy Barnett observes, "This is important. In our denomination, there are so many older pastors, and they need help."[75] Just as

---

[74] Russell and Bucher, *Transition Plan*, 47.

[75] Interview with Tommy Barnett, April 30, 2015.

importantly, these seasoned pastors can *give* help. They have the unique opportunity to help the board and congregation embrace a younger leader, preferably one who has a history with the church and has been mentored by the veteran.

Although there is no one-size-fits-all model, every plan should include specific role expectations, phases, dates, and financial considerations. The transfer of leadership should occur publicly, where the church can honor the veteran while affirming the authority of the new leader. After the transition, both successor and veteran should pursue a continuing relationship of genuine affection and mutual support.

According to Weese and Crabtree, "Succession planning is the second most important need in every church in the country (well-trained and committed pastoral and lay leadership that is culturally relevant being the first), and few if any do it or do it well."[76] We can all pray for the day when the exception becomes the rule—when "inspired leaders are

---

[76] Weese and Crabtree, *The Elephant in the Boardroom*, Kindle e-book, Location 118.

insistent that the Body grow from strength to strength and from leader to leader, rather than from avoidance to chaos; where a clear, biblically based plan is activated when leaders change; where veteran leaders mentor emerging leaders."[77]

~~~~~~~~~~~~~~~~~~~

May God grant wisdom and courage to His servants, young and old, so that what was said of Moses may be said of us: "Moses was faithful in all God's house" (Heb. 3:2). And when we have finished our course, may we, like Jesus, be able to say to our Father: "I have brought you glory on earth by completing the work you gave me to do" (John 17:4-5). Amen.

---

[77] Ibid., Kindle e–book, Location 124.

Bibliography

Adizes, Ichak. *Corporate Lifecycles: How and Why Corporations Grow and Die and What To Do About It.* Englewood Cliffs, New Jersey: Prentice Hall, 1988.

Damazio, Frank. *The Vanguard Leader: A New Breed of Leader to Encounter the Future.* Portland, OR: Bible Temple Publishing, 1994.

Dowdy, Naomi. *Moving On and Moving Up from Success to Significance: Practical Principles for Legacy Management and Leadership.* Lake Mary, FL: Creation House, 2010.

Ford, Kevin G. *Transforming Church: Bringing Out the Good to Get to Great.* Carol Stream, IL: Tyndale House Publishers, 2007.

George, J. Don. *Against the Wind: Creating a Church of Diversity through Authentic Love.* Springfield, Missouri: My Healthy Church, 2012, Kindle e–book.

Gregory, Joel. *Too Great a Temptation: The Seductive Power of America's Super Church.* Ft. Worth, TX: The Summit Group, 1994.

Lee, Wayne and Sherry Lee. *The Church Life Model: A Biblical Pattern for the Spirit-filled Church.* Lake Mary, FL: Creation House, 2011.

Lim, David. Syllabus and Class notes, PTH L 967
Apostolic Leadership in Asian Churches, Assemblies
of God Theological Seminary, October, 2011.

Rainer, Thom S. *Autopsy of a Deceased Church: 12
Ways to Keep Yours Alive.* Nashville, TN: B&H
Publishing Group, 2014.

Russell, Bob and Bryan Bucher. *Transition Plan.*
Louisville, KY: Ministers Label Publishing, 2010.

Seaward, Rick, Lecture at Victory Family Centre for
the course Apostolic Leadership in Asian Churches
(class notes for D. Min. course, Assemblies of God
Theological Seminary, Extension Class, Singapore,
October, 2011).

Simun, Phil. "Timeline of Transition Events," First
Assembly of God, Sumter, SC.

Weese, Carolyn and J. Russell Crabtree. *The Elephant
in the Boardroom: Speaking the Unspoken about
Pastoral Transitions.* San Francisco, CA: Jossey-
Bass, 2004, Kindle e–book.

Wilkes, Gene. *Jesus on Leadership.* Wheaton, IL:
Tyndale House, 1998.

About the Author

For 27 years, Dr. Terry Roberts has served as founding pastor of Trinity Church in Columbia, SC. Terry is also an executive presbyter with the Assemblies of God in South Carolina and an adjunct professor at Southeastern University in Lakeland, Florida, his alma mater. He holds an M.A. in Bible from Columbia International University, and he earned his Doctor of Ministry in church leadership at the Assemblies of God Theological Seminary (AGTS). Terry and his wife Sandra have a daughter and son-in-law and 8-year-old grand-twins.

Made in the USA
San Bernardino, CA
18 August 2018